NO *Crystal* STAIR

SHARON V. VAN ALSTYNE

ALL RIGHTS RESERVED. This book contains material protected under international and Federal Copyright Laws and Treaties. Any unauthorized reprint or use of this material is strictly prohibited. No part of this book may be reproduced or transmitted in any form or by any means, electronic or mechanical, including photocopying, recording, or by any informational storage and retrieval system without the expressed written permission from the author / publisher.

Copyright © 2021 Pixie Pan Books

First Printing

ISBN: 978-0-9672136-5-1

Printed in the United States

Published by
Pixie Pan Books
801 Dellwood Street, Ste. 100
PMB 310
Bryan, TX 77803

Visit us on the Web!
www.pixiepanbooks.com

To my three beautiful children:

Bruce, Lance, and Darlene

&

my precious grandchildren:

Ariel, Blake, Sophia, Kristopher, Yola, Lilly, Jonas, and Raina.

Contents

Foreword _____ vii

1980 _____ 1

A Little Everywhere _____ 2
Yesterday's _____ 3

1981 _____ 4

Visions of Complexity _____ 5
Lonely Shadows _____ 6
A Love Song for Me _____ 7
Searching _____ 8
Visions _____ 9
The Confines of My Mind _____ 10
Black and White _____ 11

1982 _____ 13

Space _____ 14
Napoleonic Complexes _____ 15
Dawn of Destruction _____ 16
My Son _____ 18

New Beginnings _____ 20
When Love's Gone Bad _____ 22
Merry-Go-Round of Love _____ 24
Undercover Lover _____ 25
Tus Ojos _____ 26
Satirical _____ 27
Amber Eyes _____ 28
The Farewell _____ 29
Solitude _____ 30

1983 _____ 31

Legacy _____ 32
The Goodbye _____ 33

Foreword

For as far back as I can remember, what I remember most is that my mother was almost always writing. She loved to write letters, poetry, and about the things she saw in the world. Even more so in an age of computer technology, mum still grabbed her notebook; preferring to write longhand instead of getting on a computer. For years, my mum has talked about writing a book. A book chronicling her experiences in this place she lovingly, and often, refers to as "Earth School."

As I write my thoughts down in this foreword to you, dear reader, I chuckle a bit; remembering all the colorful characters she met and knew along her life's journey, and who, through their actions, made it into "The Book." Alas, that book is still forthcoming, and in its stead an offering; a tiny selection of poetry mum has written from 1980 to 1983. I would like to take a moment, however, to tell you a funny little story that I hope will explain the title of this book. We named it "No Crystal Stair," after that wonderful poem "Mother to Son," by Harlem Renaissance poet, Langston Hughes. If you have not read this poem, I entreat you to please find a copy. You can find it on the internet. It is indeed a powerful poem.

The year was 1974, Boston, Massachusetts. I was 9 years old. My younger brother, Lance, and I were enrolled in a fine arts school in the afternoons. The Elma Lewis School of Fine Arts was a brilliant place for young children of African descent to study dance, drama, music, sewing, and cooking, etc. In our drama class, our instructor, Vernon Blackmon, gave each of us a copy of Langston Hughes's poem "Mother to Son," to take home and memorize. Mum got involved; wanting to hear our recitation, which ending up being a coaching session. She made a copy for herself; committing every line to memory in just a few days. My brother and I managed to memorize it, but mother did a lot more. The poem seemed to resonate so much more with her that she found every opportunity to recite it to us; and boy did every chance to recite it present itself. Don't have a bad day and think you were about to give up. "Son," she'd say, "life for me ain't been no crystal stair…!" and off she'd launch into the entire poem — from memory. But it was how she would recite it that was the incredible thing — as if she wrote it and deliver it with such passion and emotion that there was not a dry eye in the house.

I'd often muse in the days and years to come, that even the great Langston Hughes, upon hearing mums recitation of his work, would turn and say… "Damn, I wrote that?" She really brought to life the struggle that many black mothers face when raising black sons, and its message that the world can be a cruel, hard place to live in, "so you better not give up!" is still an important and relevant message today. With that, I leave you to get on with reading the musings and poetry written by my mum, "The Contessa," as she was lovingly referred to in the modelling world back in the day.

Happy Reading!
B. W. Van Alstyne

"Hold fast to dreams. For if dreams die, life is like a broken wing bird that cannot fly."

… Langston Hughes

A Little Everywhere

A Little here, a little there, a little everywhere.
Giving with such great intent — what I thought was meant,
Until there was none for me to spare...

Yesterday's

Where did all my yesterday's go? I saw them so clearly just moments ago;
The hours we spent, happy and content, bring back all my yesterday's.

We cared so much, shared so much
Such laughter and such joy. Not stopping once to realize
That all our yesterday's passed by.

We look at all our memories, reliving them one by one,
And remembering all our yesterday's and treasuring each one.

Visions of Complexity

These visions from my mind reflect the complexity of my soul.
Incomprehensible, yet simplistic in their form;
Not meant for everyone to understand
But for those who take the time to see
And feel them beyond their own souls.

Does this complexity ever become easier to ascertain —
The sweet simplicity of my soul's truer meaning?

Lonely Shadows

> The shadows on the wall are from the shadows of my mind…
> Bobbing and weaving mysteriously as though blending with time;
> A time when my soul cries out from the partitions of my mind.
> These shadows show a weariness of the pain and hurt they knew
> Still bobbing and weaving mysteriously, as though blending with time.

A Love Song for Me

Of all the beautiful songs of love
Why can't there be one for me?
Someone to sing of my loveliness
And how very much I seem to mean.

My very touch, my gentleness,
Oh, sing a song for me!

I feel a song a comin'
Let your heart lead the way,
And take from me the pain I feel;
Wash it clean away.

Dry my tears with your singing
And let love take us far away…
To a mystical, magical paradise
Where love's rhapsodies and melodies play.

Searching

Searching for Understanding,
Yet no one wants to understand;
Striving to belong, yet no one
Accepting the responsibility of being.

The endless search goes on and on;
For no one is ready to admit their inadequacies.
We dare not look for the truth within ourselves;
For we are haunted by the meaning of our own existence.

So, we continue to point a finger in the other direction;
Passing along a weight we cannot carry,
And desperately long to be understood,
And loved for what, and who, we really are.

Visions

Love was just a vision in my mind;
The loving, the sharing, the happiness, and the joy.
But like a storm at sea came a flood of pain,
And hurt and disappointments.

Much like the floods that washed away the lands,
So too were my dreams and visions.
I step ahead and look back to see the waste
And destruction left behind.

Like the storm that came in the night,
So shall the calm; and time will rebuild
what the storm has washed away.

The Confines of My Mind

The Confines of my mind are heavily burdened;
Knowing that I cannot share the sadness nor weight.

The words are there,
So vivid and so stark;
Leaving me to drift alone
In the stillness and in the dark.

The mind knows, as I do, the loneliness I feel;
Cut off and shut out, and totally in the dark.

But the darkness will fade into morning,
Which will bring forth a new light,
To guide me down the right path…
I could not see last night.

Black and White

Black girl, can your eyes not see?
Caught up in a black body,
But as white as can be.

Your goals are unrealistic,
Your future already planned,
But you are far too busy playing
at Ms. Ann; to even take a
Notice of this ingenious plan.

Your own cannot accept you,
And it's easy to surmise...
For them, it seems you're all dressed up in
Your white girl's disguise.

And so, you're just left spinning,
Whirling and twirling 'round,
Trying to fit in where you can
On life's dizzying merry-go-round.

You search, and you search for a few kindred souls;
While trying to hang on to you original goals.
But those dreams are sadly fading at a much faster pace
That it has you feeling so left outy in this world's maddening race
And still, you travel down life's rocky road,
With an ever-heavy burden you look to unload.

Why don't you open up your eyes,
So, you can finally see…
And get out of that white girl's body, For you are as black as can be!

1982

Space

Space is such a sacred place --
One must guard it with pride;
Making careful selections of who you allow inside.
For once there is intrusion you're left struggling to survive.

They wear upon your consciousness,
They drain you of all you possess inside,
And leave you with such emptiness…
…while politely stepping aside.

Napoleonic Complexes

Napoleonic Complexes are more than I can bare…
which leave you with insecurities and keep you in despair.

Napoleonic Complexes are wearisome indeed,
They have you hiding feelings
And misinterpreting needs.

So full of non-committal's,
Too afraid to take a chance,
To venture on love's lonely quest
In search of sweet romance.

Napoleonic Complexes,
False images of a great plan
You've lost your all, your everything,
To prove that you're a man.

Dawn of Destruction

With Dawn came destruction,
Self-inflicted pain;
Flaming hot as if on fire,
Which poured forth her burning desire.

Searching for life's shelters while blowing them away.
Came Dawn of destruction, self-inflicted pain.

Desperation is always knocking,
While panic's in the air;
Wandering aimlessly about—
Does anyone even care?

Destruction all around you,
Shakey is your game.
With Dawn there came
destruction... ...
Self-inflicted pain.

You're weeping and you whimper,
Just like a child at play;
Chasing after rainbows that you have sent away.

With Dawn there came destruction,
Self-inflicted pain…
…fury, love, and passion were Dawn's endless game.

You search for understanding,
Yet no one can understand…
The striving to belong and take
responsibility in hand.

Your endless search goes on and on,
As faults steep in mulish persistence;
For you dare not look at them deep within
For a meaning that haunts your existence.

So, you point in another's direction
For a weight you cannot carry;
And long to be loved and understood,
Which seems quite customary.

My Son

You stand before me, my narrow one
So straight and so tall. About to leave
Your mother's nest, which has protected you for so long.

You're trying to make decisions now
You want to be a good man,
And you've had no positive role models even lending you a hand.

Inside you are afraid. It's scary starting out,
And you're not even certain what it's really all about.
The road ahead is rocky, with many paths to choose;
And if you take the wrong one, you're certain to pay some dues.

Your mother's love is strong, my son.
She'll help you along the way;
For only she and God know
The struggles you soon will face;

But they'll be there to guide you, giving
you strength, courage, and faith;
As you stumble down each path,
Making your very own mistakes.

Put your fears behind you
Take the anger from your heart,
Because anger clouds your vision and
takes from you a part...
...of that lovely blossoming person

that you're striving to be
And surges forth a monster;
Too horrifying to see.

You have some strengths and courage
To start you on your way
So, put one foot in front of the other
And you'll have it made.

Take it slowly in the beginning
And don't be afraid; think carefully,
Choose wisely and most of all my son...
...Let yourself love selectively
For you too are a chosen one!

New Beginnings

What is this feeling that erupts in my soul?
Dreaming dreams, I had thought, all but vanished long ago.

Feelings of contentment,
And a peacefulness that I know,
With a serenity that possesses me; a
blessing love can only bestow.

The choices of all man's phrases
will never ever do… When
expressing my true feelings And
love I have for you.

For the love we share can't be compared to
any love I've ever known…
…We'd nurtured it so beautifully;
'til love blossoms were fully grown.

With each new bud that begins to sprout, on
fingered branches of life's tree,
Entwined as one, as we both are,
A beautiful sight to see.

Still growing in love,
Building castles of sand, upon life's rocky
shore, sharing new beginnings, just living our
life -- even better than before.

Let us make this one promise,
Sealed tight with a kiss,

Not to take us for granted,
Then our days shall be bliss.
I promise to honor the love I feel today
And watch it flourish and grow
Showing other's along the way.

A much happier existence,
And a peacefulness I know;
It's a brand brand new beginning;
And it's beginning to show!

When Love's Gone Bad

When you first came into my life,
You were still living with your wife.
"Our love had gone bad," is what you had said.
But she is still able to mess with your head.

Oh baby, this love of ours simply won't do;
She's got hold of your mind and has your body too!

As each new day passes, still growing apart,
That it started you thinking of making a new start.
You gave her your love, without reservation—
Then you watched her abuse it without hesitation;
Our love simply won't do,
She's got hold of your mind and has your body too.

Then you told me you didn't love her,
You didn't care anymore,
So, why can't you tell her?
Just walk out the door.

Why go on pretending in each other's lives;
When there are no more real feelings, or positive vibes?
My love still runs deeper than you'll ever know,
Why can't you just give up, let the other love go?
For this is the reason our love simply won't do;
She's got hold of your mind and has your body too.

You had thanked me before, do you remember? I can,
For restoring your life and feeling more of a man.
So, why do you let her keep leading you astray and
destroy precious love; throwing it all away?

And that is why our love simply won't do.
She's got hold of your mind and has your body too!

Merry-Go-Round of Love

Love has let you down
And has your head turned completely around,
Never knowing which way is up or down;
A victim of love's merry-go-round.

Don't just go along for the ride,
Get off, and deal with your feelings inside.
You can't go wrong if you just try;
For love is something you just cannot hide.

It's clear to see that your love is true; although
he's given up on you; for vows were shared with
his love of another — yet still he wants you for
his lover.

Feelings of confusion come into view,
And you're left wondering just what to do;
Should he have his cake and eat it too?
Or simply deny him as he's denied you.

Love is just a merry-go-round;
That has your head spinning
'Round and 'round.

Undercover Lover

I never liked being the "other lover."
It's so cut and dry and so undercover;

You settle for less than second best,
Because somebody else will have all of the rest.
It's just so tuff being the "other lover."
It's so cut and dry, and so undercover.

And all the while he says, "he don't care," You
can't help but notice that he is still there; still
giving him all of what you feel inside; while
stroking his ego and restoring his pride.
It's just so tuff being the "other lover..."
It's so cut and dry, and so undercover.

Hoping your future's safely cupped in his hands,
You're soon to find out that he's got other plans;
Why would he leave his comfortable nest...
When he's got you both, and all of the rest;

A man would be crazy to leave all his girls;
For he's got the best of both possible worlds.
Yeah, I never liked being the "other lover..."
It's so cut and dry, and so undercover.

Tus Ojos

When I had gazed into your beautiful eyes
You wore a covering, and not a disguise;
But I could still see the very depth of your soul,
Which left me to ponder its truth as a whole;

In its crystal clarity of stories untold,
Your eyes are like windows—to watch stories unfold.
I take a second look; what is this that I see?
And with clear understanding, you're no mystery;

Your body language leaves you with nothing to hide,
But I still am intrigued by what your eyes hold inside.

Satirical

Most men's brain is like their third leg.
You know the one I mean--
It hangs down and comes to attention—
when they want to impress.

Are there no feelings running through those veins?
Such insensitive playthings.
Trying to score at child's games;
Yet afraid of life's real conquest.

A sad state of affairs, this game of love…
That brain being man's third leg.

Amber Eyes

Beyond your eyes lay hidden depths
That only a few shall know, Such
fascinating tales to tell, such
tenderness to show.

The clever eyes of a sly ole fox That
pierce the starry night, in ambered
brilliance, encompassing all,
They shine like a candlelight.

Your eyes reflect like mirrors of a soul
I've always known, and with every
passing glance we share,
We feel so all alone!

Allow me one indulgence,
And if you feel it wise,
That I'd love to know the man that dwells
Behind those amber eyes.

The Farewell

To think I really loved you,
To think how much I cared,
That you thought I was never that special,
And I thought you were never that fair.

You stirred up all those feelings,
Too deep for you to know;
Feelings that I had tucked away So
very long ago.

You led to believe that this was
more than just a fling; to keep me
tied up and a dangling; like a
puppet on a string.

To think I really loved you,
To think how much I cared,
That you thought I was never that special,
And I thought you were never that fair.

Solitude

Share with me in solitude a moment of silent bliss;
listening and rising with gladness, from the depths
of a dark abyss.

Sleep not in the waking hours,
Carefully thinking your choices through, For,
so precious are these moments spent—
In silence, alone with you.

A universal language speaks,
It's unmistakably clear; that's if
only one would listen close Then
they would surely hear.

The rise and fall of love's rhythmic breath—
Still echoes in the air—
creating moments of silent solitude;
So precious for us to share.

1983

Legacy

(A dedication to my children)

When I look at you, my children,
All that I can see—
Are visions of such loveliness;
Extensions of me,

Each of you is special, in many wonderful ways;
Making your mark in this cruel, hard world,
Getting the most from your today's.

It is rarely ever spoken
For this, I know is true;
That sometimes I get all caught up worrying over you.
So, let me go on record for what I'm going to say…
For I only want what's best for you — the best in every way!

The Goodbye

It seems we barely say hello, before
it's time to say goodbye; trying to
hang on to this grain of time and
trying hopelessly not to cry.

Holding on so desperately
For one more lingering kiss,
Savouring the passion—
And moments of true bliss.

Caressing arms enfold me.
Hanging on for dear, sweet life.
Afraid you'll take your arms away
And my heart will know such strife.

Each moment gets more precious
Then the time we knew before That
it seems we barely say hello
When you're walking out the door.

Let the smell of your sweet love, my dear,
Remain upon my breast, And
I'll cling to it forevermore
Just knowing I've been so blessed.

If ever there were a way, my love
that I could step through time; I
would stop it at 'hello.' and then,
we'd never say goodbye!

www.ingramcontent.com/pod-product-compliance
Lightning Source LLC
Chambersburg PA
CBHW062243300426
44110CB00034B/1921